PHILADELPHIA EAGLES

BY MARV ALINAS

The Child's World
childsworld.com

The Child's World
childsworld.com

Published by The Child's World®
800-599-READ • childsworld.com

Photography Credits
© ChrisFloresFoto/Envato: football texture; Chris Szagola/AP Photo: 10–11, 15; Damian Strohmeyer/AP Photo 17; Daniel Kucin Jr./AP Photo: 19; David J. Phillip/AP Photo: 21; Denis Kennedy/AP Photo: 12–13; Derik Hamilton/AP Photo: cover, 2; Joe Robbins/AP Photo: 7; oasisamuel/Shutterstock.com: 6, 9, 15 (football); Perry KnottsAP Photo: 4–5

ISBN Information
9781503875159 (Reinforced Library Binding)
9781503875500 (Portable Document Format)
9781503876545 (Online Multi-user eBook)
9781503877580 (Electronic Publication)

LCCN
2024952243

Printed in the United States of America

BRINGING THE WORLD TO YOUNG READERS 1968

ABOUT THE AUTHOR

Marv Alinas has written dozens of books for children. When she's not reading or writing, Marv enjoys spending time with her family and traveling to interesting places. Marv lives in Minnesota.

Philadelphia Eagles quarterback Jalen Hurts

CONTENTS

The Team

The Philadelphia Eagles are a football team. They play in Philadelphia, Pennsylvania. The team started in 1933.

The Philadelphia Eagles run onto the field to play football.

The Colors

Their team colors are green, silver, and black. Their **mascot** is an eagle. His name is Swoop.

Swoop is known for doing crazy stunts!

Swoop was first seen in 1994.

The Conference

The Eagles are in the NFC East. The NFC stands for National Football **Conference**. There are three other teams in the NFC East.

The Dallas Cowboys, the New York Giants, and the Washington Commanders are also in the NFC East.

The Stadium

The Eagles play at Lincoln Financial Field. It is a big **stadium**. It opened in 2003. It can hold more than 67,000 people.

Concerts and other events are also held at the stadium.

The Football Field

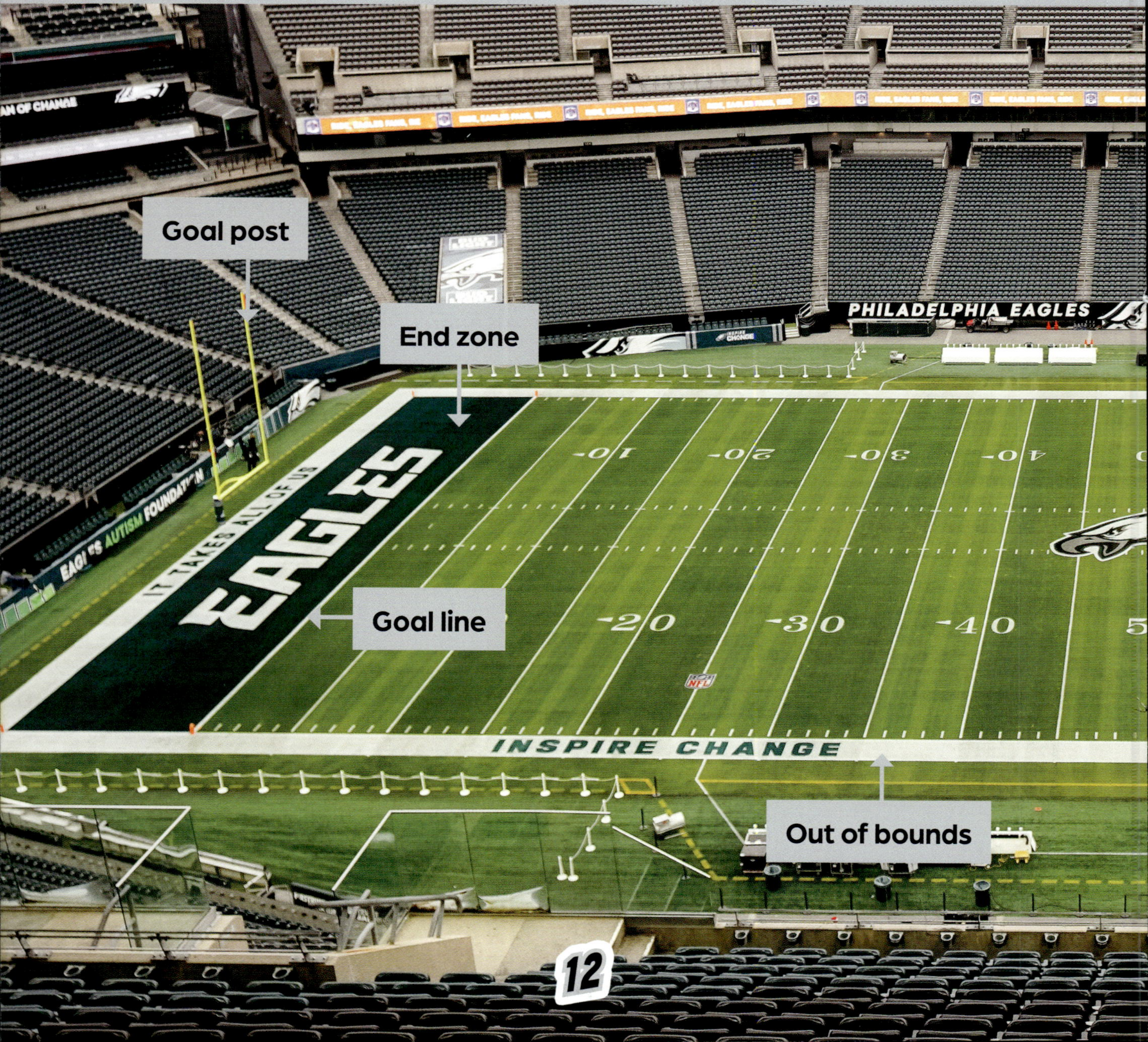

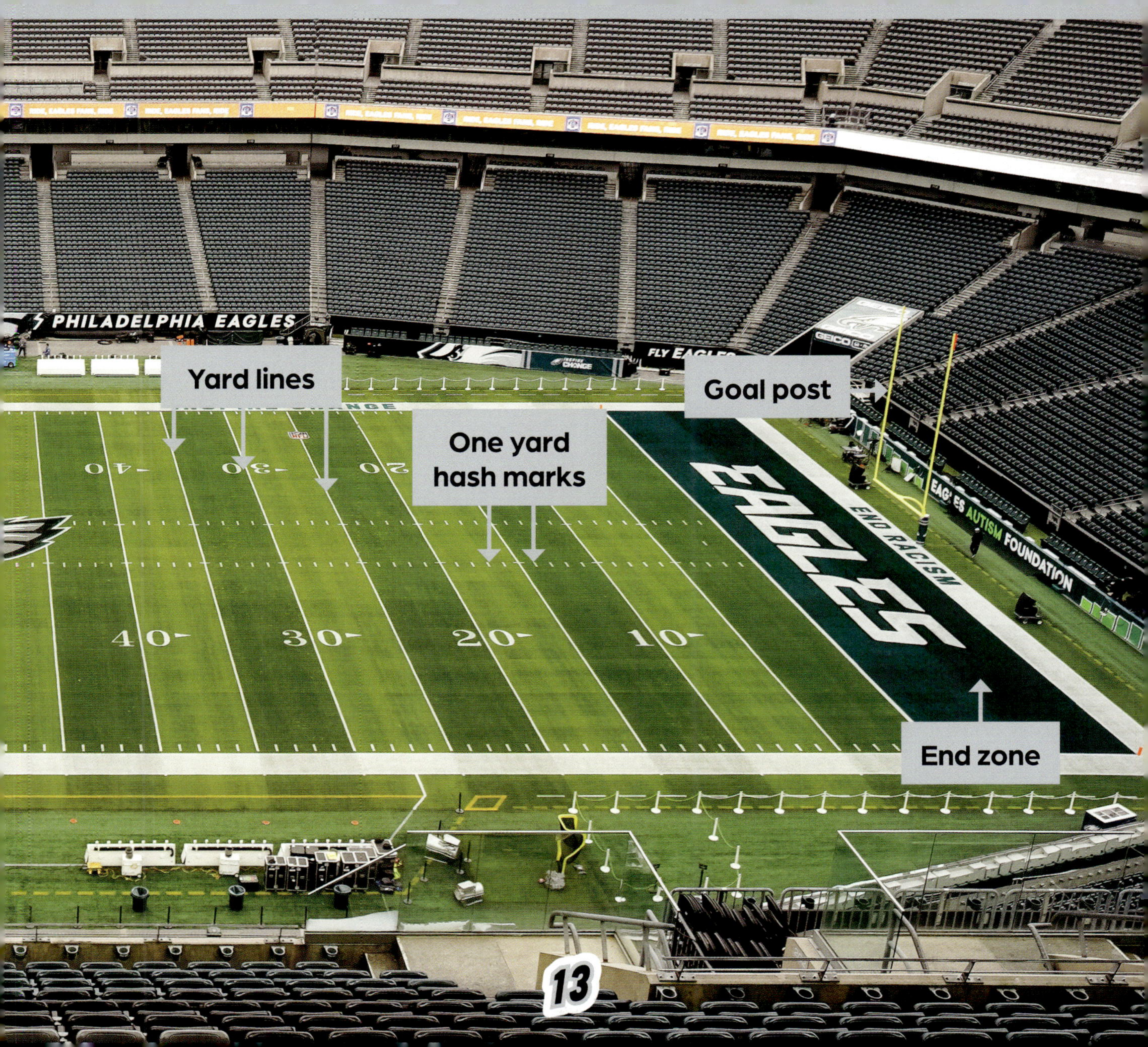
PHILADELPHIA EAGLES
Yard lines
Goal post
One yard
hash marks
EAGLES
END RACISM
End zone
40
30
20
10

Fun Fans

Fans of the Eagles love to wear the team's colors. Many people wear a **jersey** with the number of their favorite player. After an Eagles touchdown, fans sing a song. It is called "Fly Eagles Fly."

Fans also love to chant "E-A-G-L-E-S . . . EAGLES!" to cheer for their team.

The Coaches

The Philadelphia Eagles have had 24 head coaches since they began. Nick Sirianni is the current coach. He has been the head coach since 2021.

Nick Sirianni worked for 3 other teams before the Eagles.

The Players

Many great players have been part of the Philadelphia Eagles. Some past greats include Donovan McNabb, Randall Cunningham, and Jason Kelce.

Current Eagles stars are Jalen Hurts and A.J. Brown.

A.J. Brown and Jalen Hurts celebrate a great play.

They are exciting to watch during games.

The Future

The Eagles have gone to the **Super Bowl** five times. They have won twice. They will keep trying for another win!

The Eagles last won the Super Bowl in 2025.

FAST FACTS

- The Philadelphia Eagles play in Philadelphia, Pennsylvania.
- The team is in the NFC East.
- Lincoln Financial Field can hold more than 67,000 people.
- The Philadelphia Eagles have won the Super Bowl twice.

GLOSSARY

conference (KON–fur–enss): In sports, a conference is a grouping of teams.

jersey (JUR–zee): A jersey is a shirt sports players wear.

mascot (MAS–kot): In sports, a mascot is an animal, person, or thing that represents a team.

stadium (STAY–dee–um): A stadium is a large building where sports and concerts are held.

Super Bowl (SOO–pur BOWL): The Super Bowl is the championship game of the NFL.

FIND OUT MORE

In the Library

Anderson, Josh. *Philadelphia Eagles.* Parker, CO: The Child's World, 2023.

Klepeis, Alicia. *The Philadelphia Eagles.* Minneapolis, MN: Bellwether Media, 2024.

Whiting, Jim. *The Story of the Philadelphia Eagles.* Mankato, MN: Creative Education, 2025.

On the Web

Visit our website for links about the Philadelphia Eagles:
childsworld.com/links

Note to Parents, Caregivers, Teachers, and Librarians: We routinely verify our web links to make sure they are safe and active sites. So encourage your readers to check them out!

INDEX